WELLS IN PICTUR

Copyright © Roger Arguile.

This edition 2021 published by Poppyland Publishing, Lowestoft, NR32 3BB.

www.poppyland.co.uk

ISBN 978 1 909796 86 7

Designed and typeset in 10.5 on 12.6 pt Minion Pro.

Printed by Ashford Colour Press.

The photographs which make up this collection come from numerous sources. Many have been reproduced so often that it is impossible to know if, and where, rights might be held. The majority were taken between 1969 and 1979, most of them in 1970, by Richard Shackle of the Norfolk Library Service; they are now in the archive of Wells Local History Group for whose assistance I wish to express my grateful thanks. Many others come from John Tuck's considerable collection of over 2000 photographs. A number of those included were taken by Betty Tipler between 1968 and 2006. Others come from photographs submitted to the Facebook group Wells—Down Memory Lane while some are from my own collection. I am grateful for permission to use them.

I am also indebted to Linda Gower . Her contemporary photographs show the town as it was at the time of publication. As for the information about the buildings, much of it comes from Mike Welland's prodigious researches into the history of the buildings of Wells over many years. For his assistance I am deeply grateful.

Where possible photographs have been credited in the caption.

Front cover: Wells next the Sea Quayside, August 2013 (Motoral1987 under CC BY-SA 3.0).

WELLS IN PICTURES
THEN AND NOW

Roger Arguile

POPPYLAND
PUBLISHING

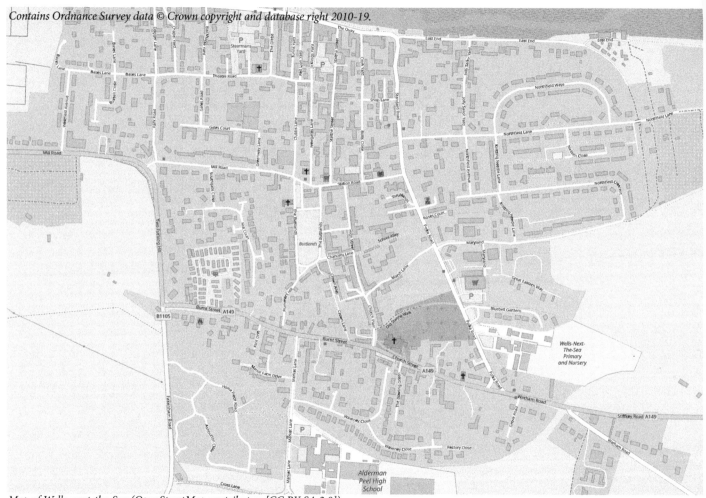

Map of Wells-next-the-Sea (OpenStreetMap contributors [CC BY-SA 2.0]).

Introduction

Wells-next-the-Sea has become a much sought after holiday resort, so much so, that many of those who come on a holiday aspire to buy a place in the town so that they can visit whenever they want to get away. Its attraction is, in good part, due to its past as port, fishery and industrial town.

The fishing still continues though it has changed its character over centuries. Its major fishery is shellfish—crabs, lobsters and pre-eminently whelks. When the first written record of its fishing appeared in 1337 its thirteen boats probably fished either by line or net for anything there was: herring, cod and their allies, rays, even eels. Fish migrate as they wish and competing fishing boats—from different countries—must follow them as they can. Thus in the 15th century there grew up the vast industry of cod fishing, first in the middle of the North Sea and then around Iceland. In those days, the decline of both the herring and cod industries had little to do with scarcity but with the mysterious movements of fish. Most of all it was to do with territorial disputes and war.

The same boats that went for fish might make a living by trade. By the 16th century, Wells vessels were routinely importing coal from the northeast of England while returning with grain, barley, malt and wheat, to provide for the expanding population in ports and towns of the mining districts. The trade was regular and important.

Wells was also a Norfolk country town serving an agricultural county based on sheep farming and barley growing. The sheep fertilised the thin soil and provided cheese, fleece, meat and wool. The barley led to a successful trade in malt. By the 18th century, one third of exported malt passed through Wells. By the 19th century, malt production had become an important industry within the town.

The signs of this industrial past are less visible than they once were having disappeared in the last fifty years. Up until the 1990s, there was much evidence of the town's past as a port, a manufactory of malt and a processor of animal feed.

The pages that follow are intended to give some visual clues as to what it looked like in times past and how it came to be as it is.

A steamer is taken out to sea by the steam tug Marie, while a sailing vessel sits against the Quay in 1901.

A Port

The importance of the harbour to overseas vessels, as well as, those along the coast can be seen on historic charts. Lucas Waghenaer's chart of 1586, shows Wells to be, along with Blakeney, an important port. By 1750, trade with the continent was significant. Wells was the second biggest exporter of malt to the continent with one third of all trade in the product going to Holland.

By the 19th century, Wells not only had several dozen colliers and fishing vessels, but also built these ships in some numbers. While most were up to 120 tons, it occasionally built larger vessels of over 300 tons. All were wooden sailing ships, carrying three and occasionally four masts. Shipbuilding never advanced to steel hulls or steam power.

Steam powered vessels began to make their appearance in the port by the turn of the 20th century. A steam tug, the *Marie,* was the last of a number and would tow both steam and rigged ships in and out of the harbour, saving valuable time and making entry into the harbour much safer.

Lucas Waghenaer's 16th century chart showing Wells and Blakeney (north is to the right).

Sailing vessels lining the quay in 1880—brigs, schooners, ketches and a steam tug, the Provider.

3

The coming of the railway, in 1857, was supposed to enhance the viability of the port. A tramway from the station was built to enable cargoes to be shipped from the holds of vessels into waggons. Hauled by horses, these would be taken to the end of the quay for onward rail transport to London and the south, or, to breweries in the Midlands. While vessels could become stormbound, the railway could carry cargo faster and in any weather.

Steamers dominated the quayside and, in wartime, they would show their advantage. Oil had to be imported whereas coal was in abundance. *Vic 55*, built during the Second World War for just that reason, was the last steamer to enter Wells harbour. Her final trip to Wells was in 1979.

Waggons hauled by horses along the Quay (Tuck).

Vic 55 was still entering the harbour as late as 1979 (Walker).

Steam vessels 1917.

Piles of beet on the quay in November 1933. From the Times newspaper with the headline 'Return to Prosperity'.

Grange's lorries load a vessel via chutes, something which could be done at low tide.

Between the two world wars various attempts were made to revive the harbour. In 1933 a British Sugar Corporation agreed to take sugar beet from local farms and, for a couple of years, it lay on the Quay in huge piles during the autumn months. Despite the attempts of the Urban District Council to get it to continue, the trade came abruptly to an end in 1935.

The Second World War brought a virtual end to the coastal trade except for a consignment of cement destined for the airfield at Egmere styled North Creake.

After the war, trade remained slow. Methods of loading and unloading relied upon muscle power. Sacks of grain were taken by barrow along a narrow plank to be emptied into the hold.

Loading in the 1950s carrying sacks on barrows.

Even post war there were still some sailing boats. Among them were the spritsail barges belonging to the Everards company of Greenhithe, named latterly after members of the family. The Alf Everard and the Ethel Everard were regular visitors to the harbour.

M.V. Nederland in September 1964 with 380 tons of Kainit fertiliser in paper sacks. It would take out 400 tonnes of barley.

A post-war revival was brought about by the use of artificial fertilisers and animal feed. It was remarkable in both its scale and suddenness. In 1964, there were 34 cargos arriving; by 1967, 73 vessels came into the harbour. In 1982, there were 258 inward shipments.

It brought employment to the town. Men gained work loading and unloading vessels; some took to joining the crew, some just for one trip some for several.

Bulk cargoes were often unloaded manually with shovels; the holds had to be fully emptied and swept before another cargo could be loaded. Such as the number of vessels that, on some spring tides, there would be as many as 8 vessels double-banked in the harbour.

Ships could only be unloaded while against the quay wall, so vessels might have to tie up alongside another vessel to await the the unloading and loading of the nearer vessel. Later, most vessels left 'in ballast', in other words, empty.

The scene from the Granary in 2021 (Arguile).

View from the Gantry of the Granary, eight coasters moored.

When a boat arrived offshore its skipper would radio the pilot. Generations of pilots guided vessels into the port, climbing on board from the pilot boat. Most recently, it was the *Ni-Tricia* that guided vessels in, sometimes turning a vessel round in the narrow channel by pushing with its bow. It was a curious craft, a steel boat built in a Chesterfield back garden by its owner, Nigel Hingley.

A pilot with local knowledge was necessary as the channel was narrow and was constantly changing. Sometimes vessels, trying to get in on an earlier tide, found themselves aground having to wait until the next tide. Occasionally, skippers would understate the draught of their vessel in an attempt get in earlier. They might end up sitting on the sand having to wait for a much later flood tide. Grounding could cause damage, for example, to the rudder, which on occasion might have to be welded up between the tides. This was much cheaper than extensive repairs requiring a dry dock.

The Ni-Tricia towing a coaster into the Quay stern first (Tuck).

The Klaas I awaiting the tide sometime in 1987 (Seeley)

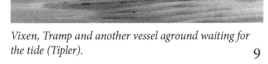

Vixen, Tramp and another vessel aground waiting for the tide (Tipler).

9

The harbour was busy throughout the year but especially in the autumn when fertiliser was required. Vessels came from Holland, Germany (both west and east), Scandinavia and Denmark and, occasionally from elsewhere in the British Isles. Regular visitors were ships owned by the Sully brothers. All were named 'Subro' with a second name beginning with 'V': *Subro Valour*, *Subro Viking* and so on. The Everards' vessels following a similar pattern. Their vessels had names ending with 'ity', for example, *Agility*.

Loading Subro Valour; harbourmaster, 'Chick' Smith (extreme right) (Whittaker).

The methods used for loading cargo improved. The 'grab' on the end of a mobile crane was a favourite, though it created for a great deal of dust, which was not appreciated by some residents. A tarpaulin attached to vertical girders alleviated the problem to some degree. Elevators were also used for loading. Another method was the suction hose, which hung from the gantry of the Granary run by Favor Parker of Stoke Ferry. It caused less dust, but often became clogged.

Some vessels became old friends. The *Tramp*, registered at Thyboroen in Denmark, made over 80 trips into the harbour. Its captain, Francis Moeller married a local girl. Its fiftieth trip was celebrated in the town with a small presentation. After the *Tramp* was lost at sea, Moeller brought his new boat, the *Othonia*, which came into the harbour just to visit the place.

right: Bob Newstead, pilot 'Boy' Court, Cpt. Francis Moeller, Brian Barker shipping agent and mayor Myrtle French.

10

left: Unloading by grab with tarpaulin wind shield 1980s (Barker).

The trade became more and more specialised towards the end of the 1980s. The few exports and imports consisted mostly of soya.

The end came suddenly in 1992 when the last motor vessel entered the harbour. Vessels were getting larger and the harbour was silting up. Favor Parker withdrew from the town; regulations became tighter and farmers' needs had changed. The Dutch sailing barge the *Albatros* soldiered on for a few years before being converted into a quayside restaurant.

From now on it would be mostly fishing vessels that would line the harbour wall.

Double-banked vessels in the 1980s—and a full car park.

below left: The Albatros in her days as a quayside pub and restaurant 2018.

below right: The Quay with Granary converted into flats 2020 (Gower).

The Quay

1324. The Quay, Wells.

At the turn of the 20th century, as the port declined, so malting seemed to boom. In 1904, the huge building, called the Granary, was built. As the port declined the quayside changed. The scaffolding poles of the new build can be seen behind the railway trucks in this picture.

The Granary, and its environs, so iconic and so dominant, merit more than a second glance.

Built by F and G Smith in 1904, the Granary was intended to store barley and malt ready for export to overseas and the British market. After the closure of their own maltings, further down the quay, in 1929, Vynne and Everett rented the building with an option to purchase.

In 1961, they sold out to Favor Parker, feed merchants of Stoke Ferry. It was this company that serviced post-war trade, importing animal feed and fertiliser up and down the coast. A business that continued until 1992.

The quayside, which had originally consisted almost entirely of industrial buildings and public houses, was cleared as this coastal trade began to develop during the 1950s.

Almost all these buildings have been knocked down being replaced by amusement arcades and fast food outlets in more recent times.

The 19th century quayside.

left: 1920s.
above: 1992.

13

A good example is the fate of a former malting bought by Vynne and Everett before the First World War. It still stands, though you would scarcely recognise it. In 1959, it was bought by Charles Platten, together with the old *Sun Inn* (seen on the left of the picture to the right). He converted the old malting into a 'Milkobar' and amusement arcade, eventually replacing the frontage and adding a flat roof (see middle right).

French's fish shop, to the right of the malting, did not and, has not, changed much. Further along, stood the huge garage, belonging, post-war, to Grange's hauliers (see below left). In 1959 it became Styman's delicatessen. Styman's originally had a shop in Freeman Street and their move to the Quay was only short lived. The building's plate glass windows might have replaced the huge doorways of the garage, but the building itself, with its chamfered sides, remained intact and stand proud of the adjoining terrace (see below right).

top: Vynne and Everett's former malting pre 1914.

middle: Flat roof and shop front to the old maltings in 2021 (Gower).

left: Grange's garage in 1959 before conversion.

right: Styman's grocers on the Quay in the 1960s.

Change has happened imperceptibly. The dour forbidding aspect of the quay's industrial buildings was relieved only by Sepping's double bay windows. His butchers' shop was the first to be altered reusing the old building for another purpose.

Sam Abel's garage was established after the war—by the remodelling of the east corner of Staithe Street and then, by the wholesale demolition of the corner in the 1970s, the roadway was widened.

top: The Quay front between the wars either side of Staithe Street.

middle: Post-war Abel's Garage, newly painted white, changed the look of the Quay. Parked cars were another change.

left: The upper bay window remains but all below is changed (Tipler).

right: A completely new corner to Staithe Street in 2021 (Gower).

15

Fishing

Whelkers at the turn of the century by Tugboat Yard, East Quay.

Although the fishing industry has left few buildings today, it seems sensible to explain how the present fishing fleet came into being.

Wells was a fishing port from, at least, the 14th century. By the 15th century, its men were bringing back salted and dried cod from Iceland. The herring fishery, dominated by the Dutch in the 16th century came and went. Oysters were dredged in the 19th century. But it was the whelk fishing which came to prominence in the 20th century.

Initially casting over the side, one at a time, a system developed of attaching the pots to each other, in shanks of eighteen or more with an anchor at each and, a 'Dan' buoy on the surface so that they could be hauled up one by one.

As long as rope was made from a natural fibre it would easily rot in sea water so both pots and rope would be coated in tar. A pot of tar gently boiling in the whelk sheds was a normal sight.

Hauling by hand was hard and may have been the cause of the large numbers of septic hands treated by the hospital in the 1930s. It was for this reason that petrol driven engines, often taken from cars, were introduced. Eventually, hydraulic hauling would take the strain, though pots still had to be lifted onto a steel table to be emptied, rebaited and stacked ready to be dropped back into the sea. Undersized whelks would be dropped back over the side, together with the odd hermit crab, while the whelks' natural prediator, the much hated starfish, would be left on the deck to dry out and die.

Bringing bags of whelks ashore at the East End before World War I.

Pots were once made of hazel and weighed down with iron bases called 'music' because they resembled musical staves. Later these were replaced by iron frames, supplied by local foundries and blacksmiths. The pots would be bound with tarred rope. Their manufacture and repair was a routine occupation for fishermen when on shore. (Modern pots are square, made of plastic and are weighed down with concrete.)

left: Jack, Billy and Jimmy Cox mending whelk pots.

below left: 'Gully', Reg and Rolly Grimes at sea sieving whelks.

below right: Alan Cox dropping re-baited pots into the sea.

Wells in Pictures

The whelks would be sieved and bagged at sea, then, brought ashore to be boiled in large boilers in the whelk sheds at the east end of the town. This procedure was judged to be unhygienic under European regulations and the whelks had to be taken to a facility in Kings Lynn. The newspaper cartoon (below) reflects the attitude of local fishermen to this change in process having been used to dealing with them for many years.

Bags were eventually replaced by plastic boxes, which were easier to handle, could be lifted, stacked five or six high by hydraulic lift, and driven away on a flatbed lorry.

above: Whelks in boxes ready to be carted to the factory in Kings Lynn (Arguile).

right: Local sentiment expressed in the Eastern Daily Press to the European Commission's food hygenie directive in 2000. The caption read, 'So I say ter Francois here if yure so keen to shove yer snout into the Norfolk whelk industry, why not do it properly?' (Archant).

opposite left: 'Loady' Cox with a basket of whelks (Tuck).

opposite right: Stanley Frary boiling whelks (McNab-Grieve).

'William Edward' and 'Sally' with the Grimes and Jordan families unloading 1960 (Jordan).

The boats themselves had scarcely changed in decades. Built of wood, they were powered by a single lug sail and oars. If the wind died, the crew could beach the boat, walk home and go back for it on the next tide. When engines began to be fitted, it meant rebuilding the stern post, however, this improvement gave greater range and reliability.

The next step was to use retired Liverpool class lifeboats, such as the *Ann Isabella* and the *Spero II*. Still built of wood, they were stronger and had more powerful engines. They lasted fifteen or more years before the next stage of development: larger boats made of different materials.

The 'William Edward' built in 1950 in full sail.

Former lifeboat Spero II with whelks being unloaded onto East Quay.

Boats looking for a different catch were several trawlers from Kent, the *Romulus*, the *Remus*, *Cortina* and the *Faustulus*, in search of sprats and rays. Though no bigger than the whelk boats, they were enclosed and operated in pairs—sailing side by side. With a trawl net strung between them, they brought in a huge numbers of the small fish. The catches were sent to Grimsby to be made into fish meal. Long before he came to Wells, this system had gained its inventor, and one of the skippers, Alf Leggett, the MBE*. The four trawlers stayed in Wells after the sprats disappeared.

Wooden boats would soon become a minority. The *William Edward's* hull was used as a mould for a GRP (Glass Reinforced Plastic or fiberglass) boat, the *Blucher*. John Nudds was the first local fisherman to buy a GRP boat of new design, the *Isabelle Kathleen*. New designs were made possible by the use of this new material and, eventually, boats with twin hulls vessel would appear, including the much larger *Nell Diana*.

Cortina, one of the Faversham trawlers.

The Blucher, a GRP boat made from a mould of the William Edward.

* Member of the Order of the British Empire.

New generation of fishing boat the Nell Diana which arrived in 2020 (Arguile).

John Nudds' boat, Isabelle Kathleen.

Wells was, until the latter part of the 20th century, an industrial town and, for a third of that time engaged in processing grain into malt. This involved germinating cereal by soaking it in water, and then halting the process by kiln drying.

Malting has existed in the town from the 16th century but much of the process had taken place on farms. Commercial malting in the 19th century occurred with the wider use of hops, which acted as a preservative as well as adding to the flavour of beer. As a result, beer could be transported greater distances. Gradually the town maltings were purchased by merchants from maltsters. From the late 1870s these businesses were consolidated by F and G Smith of Great Ryburgh. The Smiths had plants in Dereham and Great Ryburgh but made their headquarters in Wells.

As consumption of beer began to fall in the 20th century, production had to be rationalised and, overnight, the Wells estate was closed. In 1929, after hundreds of years of malting, Wells was left with a dozen or so empty maltings and stores. No one, it seemed, knew what to do with these huge buildings and, gaunt and foreboding, they were allowed to decay.

Staithe Street maltings in 1970 (Shackle).

Some of the buildings did find other uses, for example, as grain stores or other agricultural related activity. Vynne and Everett, grain merchants of Swaffham, came to Wells early in the century. Expanding in the 1930s they took, among other buildings the famous Granary on the Quay. In 1941, the Staithe Street maltings were taken over by the Eastern Counties Farmers Cooperative (ECFC) with headquarters in Ipswich. Pauls Malt, also founded in Ipswich in 1842, came to the town in the same year, while Favor Parker came in 1961.

All have gone.

This composite picture, from photographs taken in the 1970s, shows the extent of the Eastern Countries estate.

The Eastern Counties Farmers Cooperative had first established a presence in Wells in 1935. Its Staithe Street premises was expanded during the war when their Yarmouth plant in was destroyed by enemy bombing. Apart from providing seed, selling grain and other produce on behalf of their members, farmers in the district, they also manufactured animal feed and sold farm machinery. Their aim was to provide a comprehensive service. Wells was geographically remote from their base and they pulled out on the town in 1971.

The yard is shown clockwise where it fronts onto Staithe Street (Shackle).

The pictures above show a 'panoramic' view of the ECFC plant taken from Staithe Street. Going clockwise (from the south) it shows the large malting (with the canopy and water tanks), adjacent to Sun Yard, and their offices. The present malting can be seen in the background above the gate pillar.

The tallest building in Wells in earlier years seen from the beach bank.

The Sun Yard malting in 1975 (Shackle).

The larger malting on the ECFC site, on its western side, unlike the building on Staithe Street lay derelict for a number of years.

With its kiln roof, it had once stood so high that, together with the Paul's malting on Tunns Yard, it dominated the skyline from the sea. It lay derelict until 1979 when it was replaced by a block of flats, Malthouse Place, whose architectural design is intended to give an indication of the land's former use.

Malthouse Place which replaced it 2020 (Gower).

Wells Maltings Arts Centre 2020 (Arguile).

No 3 malting on Star Yard off Staithe Street in 1970 (Shackle).

That the other malting survived was, in part, due to central government changing its mind about Norfolk's housing requirements and resistance from the newly formed Wells Community Association and local Arts group. After nine years of fundraising the Association obtained the lease, cleared the building of rubble, pigeon droppings and rusting machinery and created a community space, with little theatre, in the building. This was the start and a project was launched in 2016 to refurbish the whole building to create a larger arts and community complex funded from the Lottery.

Of the other maltings in the town, few have survived. Only photographs remain.

Standing in Staithe Street, by the Wells maltings and looking east, is Star Yard. This used to lead to Stoughtons Yard, running down to the Quay. In Star Yard was another malting. The hoist used for lifting the sacks of barley to the upper floors can still be seen projected from the building. All gone, the yard now gives access to commercial storage facilities.

Star Yard in 2020 (Gower).

27

No. 18 Pauls malting in the 1920s.

No. 18 Pauls malting in 1970 (Shackle).

Malting No 18 seen from Red Lion Yard (Shackle).

Modern Houses on Tunns Yard 2020 (Gower).

The second most prominent malting in the town was the last to cease working. Part of it can still be seen standing on the Quay. Sometimes known as Pauls' malting, it is named after Messrs. Paul of Ipswich. Bought in 1941, after one of its works in Ipswich had been requisitioned by the Government, it was a huge enterprise and ran from the Quay up the hill almost as far as Theatre Road. The Quay frontage remained even though, following its closure in 1961, it was replaced by houses. The frontage is now given over to shops.

above right: Shop Lane looking west to a former malting (Shackle).

above left: Bolts Close showing the same building from the south (Shackle).

left: Bolts Close in 2020 (Gower).

Shop Lane from the same aspect in 2020 (Gower)

To the east of Staithe Street and running parallel is Bolts Close. On the west side stood another huge malting at the junction with Shop Lane. We can see the grain store. To the right was the steeping chamber. Here the barley was soaked to promote germination before being shovelled onto one of the three malting floors to germinate. The process was continuous. Temperature control was achieved by opening and closing the louvres. For a fortnight,the malting barley was turned each day with a malt shovel. By germination sugars would be released to make the beer. Finally there was the kiln, into which the malt was barrowed in order to stop germination and roasted. There remains now only a row of cottages, one called Malt Cottage.

29

Here a number of survivors from the past can be seen. Almost by a miracle, on the opposite side of Croft yard, the oldest identifiable malting in the town can be found. Bought by Thomas Bunting in 1584, it passed through many hands before being acquired by Smiths. In 1970, it looked very forlorn and very likely to fall down. However, today, turned into some fine town houses, it looks like it might see out its half millennium.

There are other remnants of past times. The Pop Inn and Playland, at the south end of the Beach Road, had a more serious purpose both as a malting and then, under the ownership of Vynne and Everett as a grain store. Intent upon preserving the character of the area, the extension to the north, on the site of the old coal vault, is of a similar style. The kiln to the rear, not quite visible in the photograph, also remains, but with its cowls long removed.

Buntings 16th century malting on the west side of Croft Yard in 1979 (Shackle).

Buntings Malting in 2020 (Arguile).   *Beach Road maltings in 1970 (Shackle).*   *Beach Road maltings in 2020 (Gower).*

Glebe Road marked the western end of the maltings and, along its eastern side were some of the smaller and, probably older, maltings. After closures these were used for different purposes. Tom Grange, haulier, had some of his garages there. South and up the hill, was the Marina Amusement Arcade, with its 'dodgem' cars. These have gone. At the top of the hill can be found Foundry House. It was formerly Cornish's foundry which closed in 1936.

Grange's Garage which occupied part of the site in 1970 (Shackle).

The same buildings looking North 1970 (Shackle).

Glebe Road looking south (Shackle).

Glebe Road in 2020 (Gower).

31

left: The junction of the Glebe and Theatre Road in 1970 (Shackle).

below: The same junction in 2021; Foundry House has some west facing windows (Gower).

Here we see the top of the Glebe in 1970. The photograph shows a tower from which barley was distributed to the various maltings. In the foreground are the ruins of the foundry.

The 2021 picture shows all traces of malting removed and the end wall of Foundry House with windows. The old foundry buildings have gone.

Boroughs and Strattons ran a bulk feed carrying business from a private yard, previously belonging to Smiths, in Shop Lane. Bought out by Dalgettys, they subsequently moved to Egmere on the Fakenham Road some four miles away. The name Stratton survives in the little close that runs north from it. The close opposite is named Ramms Court after a local butcher who owned land around the town.

The malting, No. 6, whose cowls can be see in the photograph, was taken down in 1988.

Boroughs and Strattons/Dalgettys entrance on Standard Road (Shackle).

Dismantling of No. 6 malting in 1988 (Tipler).

Stratton Place 2020 (Gower).

Dewing and Kersley's flour mill before about 1910—note the steam lorry.

Malting was not the only industry in the town. The milling of wheat had been undertaken for centuries. Mill Road is a clue to the half a dozen windmills that stood on the crest of the ridge running parallel to the Quay. The last to go, a smock mill, in 1904 was on the brow of the hill on Northfield Lane. Instead a huge modern mill was built close to the railway station on Maryland by Messrs. Dewing and Kersley. Its 'Sunshine Flour' was sold throughout the region. A huge grain silo was added in the 1960s. This proved to be a liability putting the company into financial difficulty. It closed in 1980. The silo remains, but the mill was demolished in 1984. The offices have become an antique shop, vet's surgery and living accommodation. The chimney was taken down after the Second World War.

Smock mill on Northfield Lane demolished in 1903.

The offices and grain silo, the mill itself gone 2020 (Gower).

The Railway

The railway came to Wells in 1857. It was intended to carry freight to and from the harbour, and agricultural produce to inland markets, thus bringing wealth to the town. The Earl of Leicester, a great agriculturalist was its major investor. A tramway opened in 1859 to carry freight to and from the Quay and ran from the station around the east side of the town to the harbour. Locomotives were not allowed on the Quay and the waggons were moved by horses (see p. 4). This improvement was supposed to improve the harbour's fortunes but the coming of the railway only hastened the decline of the port. The railway could carry freight faster, in larger quantities and was not affected by storms at sea.

The railway also brought tourists into the town. In the inter-war years, day tourists came in such numbers that enterprising folk offered a taxi service from the station to the beach. Latterly pilgrims came to Walsingham by train and the carriages were stored at Wells until they were needed for the return journey.

above: A windmill, a steam driven mill and the railway station—late 1800s (Tuck).
below: Taxis waiting to take visitors back to the station (Tuck).
left: East Quay with railway waggons (Tuck).

35

The station included the entrance and booking hall, offices, the porticoed train shed and an engine shed with a turntable.

In 1866 a second line was built to the west taking traffic to Heacham and from there to Kings Lynn. It was never that successful partly because the Heacham platform, outside the train shed, meant that transferring to the Dereham/Norwich line was not straightforward.

In 1935, the shed was demolished to make way for open platforms, each with its own canopy. The Heacham line closed to passenger traffic in 1952 and, when the line was swept away in the 1953 floods, no effort was made to restore it for goods traffic.

The station as originally built in 1857 picture taken in 1909.

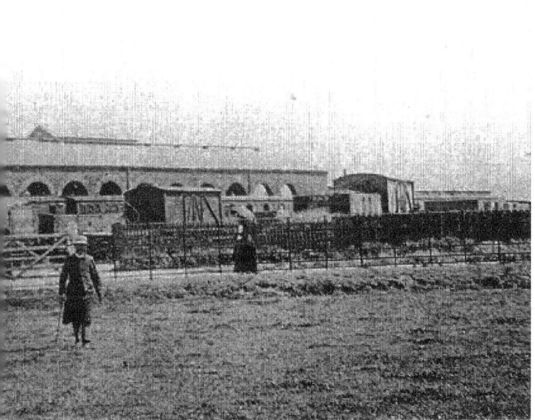

Passenger train heading towards Heacham in 1952 the year the line was closed.

The station booking hall with platform canopy in 1956.

Wells in Pictures

Diesel railcars had better acceleration than steam though the stops were as frequent.

left: Wells station in 1956.
right: The site of the station yard in 2020 (Gower).

The railway was nationalised in 1948. Diesel railcars were introduced in 1955 producing a faster service for workers travelling to Norwich or school pupils to Fakenham. It became possible to leave Wells at 6.50 am and arrive in Norwich by 8.30 am, in time to walk to one of the many factories and offices in the city.

Following the 1963 Beeching Report, the line closed on 3 October 3 1964. The vast estate of lines and sidings, replete with sheds and turntable were all to disappear within a short time. It left land for an industrial estate, which never really materialised. There are a number of industrial units, some in various states of decay, and a caravan sales park.

Two views from the same spot show how dramatically it has changed.

The station booking hall frontage was all that remained. The tracks were lifted in 1965, platforms and adjacent buildings were removed and the tramway cutting to the Quay was left bare.

The area became a blight to the town and parts of the station building were demolished.

lower left: The station partly demolished 1969 (Shackle), lower right: The harbour branch after removal of tracks (Tipler).

39

The Streets

Staithe Street

While the northern end of the town was dominated by maltings and other industrial buildings from the 19th century, there remained a large number of retail outlets. Since that period, some businesses, like bakeries, butchers and shoe shops have shrunk in number and other trades, such as those associated with horses, have disappeared.

Staithe Street (meaning Harbour) is now the main shopping street. It looks for all the world as if it has scarcely changed. Some buildings retain their characteristics and others have completely disappeared.

A good example lies towards the bottom of the hill. Shop fronts on the right hand side have only changed superficially over a hundred years while on the lefthand side, the ECFC Yard has been developed.

The picture looking south, up the hill, was taken in the 1920s. The cottage on the right, which stood just to the south of the present maltings, has disappeared. It became part of ECFC's yard, then a car park and, today, a new building stands on the spot.

At the other end of the street, on the west side, stands the grand colonnaded frontage of Leftley's grocery store. It has changed little since 1861, when Wells was a prosperous port. In 1911, after Thomas Leggett, draper, outfitter and milliner, sold it to the International Tea Stores, there was a gas explosion which nearly wrecked it. International ran it as a grocers' for many years.

After the gas explosion in 1911.

International stores in 1970 (Shackle).

Leftleys expanded premises in 2020 (Gower).

Another survivor is another former draper, Herbert Butcher, which retains its wrought ironwork balustrade and the awning. The latter would once have shaded customers browsing its wares. It is now a gift shop and a cafe.

Butchers' Drapery on Staithe Street between the wars.

The same shop 2021 (Arguile).

By contrast the upper east side of Staithe Street had quite changed. Once it was Mayshiel, the residence of the Smith family, maltsters, and had a huge garden big enough for a tennis court, a kitchen garden and stable. The garden was behind a great wall and was fringed with ilex trees.

left: Staithe Street with Mayshiel and its garden to the right (Shackle).

right: Staithe Street in 2021 (Gower).

left: Aerial view of Mayshiel garden.

right: A parade of shops in place of Mayshiel's garden (Gower).

The aerial picture shows its extent. Now a parade of shops, some of them set back from the street, fills the garden area leaving just a few token trees left to give some indication of what had been there.

The town once provided for all local needs including clothing. Wells and Son, men's and children's outfitters, had several outlets on Staithe Street. At one of the company's shops, opposite, you could pay your electricity bill. The company also took on the shop at the top of the street, now Leftley's, who took it over in 1985 (see p. 42).

Today, the presence of bollards show that the street is pedestrianised during the day. These small convenience stores find it hard to compete with supermarkets.

top: Two shops run by Wells and Son, which flourished between the wars and afterward until the 1970s.

bottom: A convenience stores and an electrical/freezer shop in 2021 (Gower).

High Street

High Street, at some time in the past, was the main shopping street. It ran down to the Church so was once known as Church Street and was, until the 1840s, the main thoroughfare out of town. (Polka Road was built about that time.) It boasted three butchers, a baker, an ironmonger, a boot and shoe maker, several tailors and outfitters, a greengrocer, a hairdresser and a musical instrument shop.

In the 1840s, a proposal to knock down the houses on one side to widen the road was never implemented. Wells' first self-service store was established here in 1949; changing hands it eventually became a freezer shop before being turned into a private house. The shops had mostly disappeared by 1970. Howells the butchers, with an adjacent hat shop, in the same ownership, was the last to go.

While some shops have left no trace, others have retained their shop fronts preserving the look of the street, if not, its character. Eade's cycle dealer's shop seen left, before the war was also a hairdresser and tobacconist. By 1970, it had become simply a hairdresser. Now it is a private house.

At the southern end of the street was Thurgur's china and glass shop, which having been there for a hundred years, closed in 1964. Empty and increasingly derelict, in 1980, it was knocked down and a new block built on the corner site.

Eade's cycle shop in the 1930s (Tuck).

Eade's hairdressers in 1970 (Shackle).

Thurgur's shop at the corner of High Street and Church Plain (Tuck).

New houses on High Street built in 1980 (Gower).

By the 1970s, the town was not merely in decline, but many of its buildings showed signs of serious neglect and decay. The conviction of Arnold Rogers, Borough Surveyor, in the 1960s, that the town needed to be modernised by building new houses seemed to be vindicated.

Some houses were demolished. Below can be seen, where a triangular building once stood, the remains of a shared chimney breast, a fireplace and the range. The chimney breast was retained and windows and a door put into the dividing wall, leaving the rest of the land as a parking place for cars.

top left: 40 High Street in 1970 (Shackle).
top right: 40 High Street in 2021 (Arguile).
bottom left: Bottom of High Street in 1969 (Shackle).
bottom right: The same building in 2021 (Ockwell).

47

Church Plain

Church Plain, at the bottom of High Street, demonstrated the dilemma of dealing with houses that had come to the end of their lives in what would become conservation areas. The Plain had some of the oldest artisan houses in the town, built at the end of the 16th century. At the northern end was Thurgurs' glass and china shop, which lay empty for years after its closure in 1964. In 1980, it was finally knocked down and replaced by new housing in keeping with the area.

The houses on the west side looked in good order in 1900, but 80 years later were in need of replacement. While the 'crowd' in this picture has been clearly posed, it still shows that the High Street now is largely empty of people. The loss of the pub, the *Eight Ringers*, the shops and of residents, means that, however well preserved the houses are, the street is empty. At night the houses are dark being mostly holiday homes.

left: *Thurgur's hardware shop closed in the 1960s (Shackle).*

above: *New houses built on almost the same footprint 2020 (Gower).*

Church Plain about 1900—locals posing for the postcard (Tuck).

Freeman Street

Freeman Street, named after its developer John Freeman, runs from the Quay to the west. The houses on the north side were built in the 1820s. It became a major shopping street.

The most dramatic changes can be seen at each end. The *Ship Inn* (left) remains intact though its licence was transferred in 1967. The cottages to its west have gone, demolished in 1962. Initially intended for housing development, only the *Ark Royal* public house was built (see p. 81). It was also demolished in 2020.

The many shops disappeared in the 1960s, though a few remain. While grocers' shops have gone some are now restaurants and other food outlets.

top : Freeman Street looking west in the 1960s.
bottom: Freeman Street in 2020 (Gower).

Freeman Street 1950s before the demolition of the Lugger Yard cottages.

Many of the fine 1820s buildings on the north side of Freeman Street remain. On the south side, one of the oldest extant houses in Wells, now called Merchant's House, stands at the corner of Blackhorse Yard. On the 1793 census it was owned by one of the most significant families in the town, the Blooms. They were a merchant family, long associated with the Normans (see p. 73).

Elsewhere a number of undistinguished houses, in a poor state of repair were demolished, and replaced by houses of similar size and character.

Something of the state of the old buildings and the yards, that ran down to the street, can be seen in this picture of the bottom of Theatre Yard, now no longer there.

top: Merchant's House in 1970 (Shackle).
middle: Part of the 1820s development on the north side.
bottom: House now demolished on Theatre Yard (Shackle).

Next to Brigg Square 1969 (Shackle).   *The same plot in 2020 (Arguile).*

51

Frank Bell at his shop doorway before WWI (Welland).

Wells once boasted a number of corner shops; Freeman Street had several. The one on the corner of Mindhams Yard was owned by a number of businesses. In its heyday it was a grocery store and an outfitters, one of whom was William Mindham. His name being given to the adjacent yard.

Mindham's grandson Frank Bell took over the business and ran it until his death in 1925. It was then taken over by the Styman brothers. They expanded in the town and in the 1950s moved out to a new store, which they converted from a garage on the Quay (see p. 14).

This shop was closed and became flats.

below left: Styman Bros shop between the wards (Welland).
below: Former shop at the bottom of Mindhams Yard 2021 (Gower).

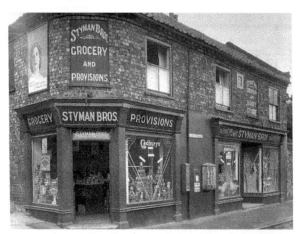

It is at the far end of the street that the most dramatic changes have taken place. The last property on the north side was Auld's—subsequently Angus's bakery. Beyond this was Barker's lorry garage. Later, Barker built a repair garage and petrol station on the site. It was demolished in the year 2000. In their place, the memory of the bakery was preserved in the name of Bakers Yard and the houses beyond, ending in a four-storey turreted building, was called Mainsail Yard.

Auld's bakery in 1970 (Shackle).

Bakers Yard and Mainsail Yard 2021 (Gower).

53

Standard Road

Standard Road is the most easterly of the three major streets running down to the Quay and is now a major thoroughfare connecting with Polka Road. The view of the Quay was once blocked by the Standard barn, where malt was stored ready for shipment. Shop Lane, a private yard leading to the numbers 1, 2 and 6 of the maltings, later gave way to the Boroughs and Strattons premises which we saw on 33. The cottage, on the immediate left of the 1920s picture, is the white building in the picture dated 1970. It was demolished in order to widen the road.

Standard Road before demolition of the barn at the end of the road 1920s.

top: Standard Road with entrance to Shop Lane 1970 (Shackle).

bottom: Standard Road in 2020 (Gower).

The change wrought by the demolition can be seen to greater effect when looking at the same buildings from the south east. The cottage below was demolished, the road widened and the east wall of what had previously been a whelk factory, behind the cottage, gained a number of windows and a doorway during its conversion into a hardware shop.

While part of the frontage was taken when widening of the road, the remainder provides a display area for garden furniture and storage of compost and aggregate for the business.

The cottage demolished to widen the road.

The whelk factory became a hardware shop (Gower).

Polka Road

Horse-drawn waggons heading for the Quay northwards.

New Road, Wells.

Polka Road in the early years of the 20th century with young horse chestnuts.

Originally named New Road, it was built in 1845 to enable traffic to get to the Quay easily. Waggons that had previously gone up the narrow High Street, whose surface was not metalled, could now proceed along a wide straight road down to the Quay or to the maltings.

The young horse chestnuts now fully mature can be seen as saplings in the earlier photograph. Down the hill, the cottages near the railway station can just be seen behind some trees.

The same view as above right 2021 (Gower).

Garage on Polka Road, for many years owned by George Cain and then by Stacey Walsingham (Tuck).

Inevitably a number of garages sprang up along this road, three in all.

Cars were unreliable and mechanical repairs constantly needed. These garages repaired and sold cars, as well as, supplying petrol to customers in the town. Arguably the earliest garage, which sold petrol, was Rose's garage. Rose had an ironmongers on High Street. In 1924, George Turner Cain opened his garage further down the road. At one time the town had half a dozen petrol stations, and for a long time none at all, until in 2018, a self-service service station was built on Polka Road.

Self service station with Cooperative store adjacent (Gower).

top: Rose's Garage on Polka Road in the 1960s.

above: Rose's Court, site of the former garage 2021(Gower).

57

Clubbs Lane

Closed in 1974, the former Oddfellows Hall was converted into flats and the auditorium behind demolished (Gower).

The existence of live entertainment in the 19th century is indicated by the name Theatre Road at the top of the yards. In the 20th century, mass entertainment was provided by the cinema around the corner in Clubbs Lane.

A travelling cinema first came to Wells in 1914. Regular showings. started in 1929 in the Oddfellows Hall. In 1937 the building was converted into a cinema, later called the Regal, part of a chain. A huge auditoriium, with steel frame and made from concrete blocks, was built behind the hall as an auditorium, which extended to Newgates Lane.

Television eventually killed it and the structure was demolished 1974. It had served locals, visitors and service personnel during the war. Children's matinees were a great draw in the 1950s.

Oddfellows Hall as Regal Cinema 1960s (Tuck).

top: Newgates Lane at the back of Clubbs Lane in 1970, with cinema auditorium to the right (Shackle).

bottom: Oddfellows Court on Newgates Lane 2020 (Arguile).

59

Station Road

Station Road runs along the top of the ridge between Staithe Street and High Street. It still sports on public house and had three (see p. 78ff). It has had several banks and still has a Post Office built in 1906. It had a Methodist chapel now the library (see p. 85).

In 1855, the East of England bank opened next door to what is now Jagger's pharmacy; it would change its name successively before moving to Station Road as the London Provincial bank. It is now an opticians.

In 1884 a branch of the Fakenham Bank was opened on the opposite side of the road. It was taken over Gurneys, Birkbeck, Barclay and Buxton bank and finally, just Barclays in 1897. In 1922 it absorbed the London Provincial Bank. The building was completely demolished and rebuilt in 1963. However, the branch closed in 2019 leaving no banks in the town.

top: London Provincial Bank on Station Street c1900.

middle: Station Road 2021 with (closed) Barclays Bank on the extreme right (Gower).

bottom: Staff of the post office in 1905 (Tuck).

Tinker's Corner looking west before the post office was built.

There are many yards that run down to the Quay and to Freeman Street from Theatre Road. While all are narrow, all are very different.

Sun Yard once ran down the side of huge maltings, part of the Eastern Counties Farmers Cooperative. It characterised a feature common in Wells—being built over at the point where it opened out onto the Quay. As the name implies the property was once owned by the former *Sun Inn*. Lost during the 1960s, it became part of Platten's fish shop, as it was thought that the adjacent Jicklings Yard, which still remains, provided adequate access to the Quay.

Sun Yard with Quay beyond (Tuck)

Jicklings Yard looking out to sea (Shackle).

The former Sun Inn with entry to the yard seen from the Quay 2020 (Gower).

61

Green's fish and chip shop on Red Lion Yard (Shackle).

Red Lion Yard running down the east side of the Memorial Club.

Red Lion Yard boasted one of Wells two fish and chip shops and was run by Teddy Green. Its crooked roadway also had a house with the flying freehold, being one of two remaining in the town.

Tunns Yard by comparison was straight and ran down the side of the Pauls' maltings. In 1984, its demolition and rebuilding, left the facade of No. 18 (Pauls' malting) alone. Behind it was built a row of houses which back onto Knotts Yard.

Knotts Yard remains, though it has no street sign as no houses front on to it. The yard gives access to the backs of those in Tunns Yard. Its un-metalled state looking more like all yards did fifty or a hundred years ago.

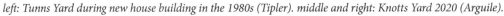

left: Tunns Yard during new house building in the 1980s (Tipler). middle and right: Knotts Yard 2020 (Arguile).

On the west side of the Glebe lay a number of yards. Only one survives today. Lugger Yard, a stub of its former self, leads to a car park. It was, for many years, a wasteland following pre-war demolition. Before that, it had been a hive of activity, the home of many poor and deprived people housed in insanitary dwellings.

Stearmans Yard, which ran parallel to Luggers Yard, survives only in the name given to a car park on the site. Rackhams Yard, Theatre Yard and Bouches Yard are marked on old maps and in some people's memories alone.

The yards were designated for improvement in 1937. Hindered by the war, a smaller area than originally planned was finally demolished in 1962. Proposals to build 67 houses, four flats and 65 garages, as well as a major road to take harbour traffic out of town, came to nothing.

above: The Busby and Gee families pose for a picture pre-WW1 (Tuck).

left: Lugger Yard following pre-war demolition (Tuck).

right: Stearmans Yard— long gone (Tuck).

63

The same fate that befell Stearmans Yard could have happened to those further west. By the 1970s, many of these yards were in a poor state. Blackhorse Yard was in a parlous state. Signs of former occupation were all too visible—ranges and fireplaces were all that was left of former houses that had been condemned as insanitary or incapable of economic repair. The yard, too narrow at its upper and lower ends for vehicular traffic, would come to look very different as these derelict buildings were replaced by extensions and new houses.

Signs of former occupation: a range downstairs and a fireplace upstairs (Shackle).

Blackhorse Yard 1970 (Shackle).

During the 1970s, land from demolished cottages were used to park cars or caravans. The latter came from the Pinewoods Holiday Camp. The camp owners did not permit caravans to remain on site permanently. They had to be removed over the winter months. It provided a minor source of income for local people who stored them in their yards during the winter.

It was individual owners who improved these yards rather than the Council. They bought up houses and their adjoining sites either refurbishing existing dwellings or by knocking several cottages into one.

Bottom end of Blackhorse Yard with stored caravans (Shackle).

The same picture in 2021 (Gower).

Dogger Lane (Tuck).

Chapel Yard, further west, was much wider. Today it gives all the appearance of having scarcely changed, but the children who once played in these streets have long gone. Even with the enlargement of some, and knocking two into one of others, they are not really suitable for bringing up a young family. They were bought by second home owners and are only occupied in the summer.

Theatre Road is named after the Fisher theatre, constructed in 1812 and one of thirteen built by David Fisher across East Anglia serving his theatre company. It closed in 1844 and was converted into housing. The building was finally demolished in 1965, leaving, on the north side, Warren's Garage, the Methodist chapel and a few houses. New housing would come.

At its west end ran Dogger Lane which remains relatively intact.

opposite: Fisher theatre converted to housing in 1844, before being demolished in 1965 (Tuck).
top, middle and bottom: Chapel Yard in 1970 (Shackle).

New Housing

Wells was ahead of many towns in providing a programme of council housing. Following pressure from Sam Peel, newly elected in 1913, building began during the First World War. The Earl of Leicester sold the land to the council and officiated at the site's dedication on Northfield Lane in 1915. There followed a row of houses on Mill Lane running westwards out of town.

Plans were made during the 1930s, which resulted in council being built houses in various parts of the town. Some schemes were delayed by the World War II, but by 1951, over 350 such houses had been built, rehousing many local families from the yards.

Mill Road house building in 1921 (French).

Mill Road houses in 1991 (Tipler).

above: Northfield Waye estate 1950s (Jordan).
opposite: Laying the memorial plaque 1915.

Historic Houses

Brigg Square, a close of houses dated to 1648 (Shackle).

The White House on Burnt Street (1970 (Shackle).

Well House on Standard Road circa 1680.

70

Wells is not noted for great houses. The aristocracy lived in Holkham and Walsingham. However, there are fine merchants' houses, some of which are, externally, almost unchanged, A small number date from the 17th century. The White House, a double-gabled property on Burnt Street, to the south of the town, is one. The close of houses on Freeman Street, known as Brigg Square, is of the same period.

Another, near the Quay, is Well House. It was probably created from a row of cottages in the 1600s. Records show it was sold in 1725 to a Wells merchant, Henry Woodrow, for the substantial sum of £150. Ownership by mariners and shipwrights makes sense given its position. A high viewing window enabled those who lived there to see when a ship was coming in.

Not all houses face the sea. Ostrich House stands behind a stone wall in Burnt Street, just a stone's throw from the Church down the hill. Dated to 1722, a new facade was added early in the next century. In 1822 it became an inn and continued to be so until the beginning of World War I.

Newgate House, now concealed behind shops on Staithe Street, was the 16th century abode of William Newgate, a considerable landowner with holdings in Holkham. The house had a brewery, malthouses and other associated buildings. We know that he bequeathed it to his widow in 1667. By the 18th century it had been leased by the banking family of Peckover. Then became the *Three Swans* public house and subsequently, the *Dukes Head*. In the 1820s three shops were built in front and, it was divided into two properties. The setback entrances to these houses can be seen between two shops today.

top: Ostrich House, sometime public house and private residence.
bottom: Newgate House, now almost invisible behind walls and houses off Newgates Lane.

71

The garden of Mayshiel in the 1920s (Tuck).

The house in 1970 when it was still a private residence (Shackle).

Now a Pet Store with flats and a coffee shop (Gower).

On the east side of Staithe Street stands Mayshiel dating from the 18th century. It was built on the once extensive property of Elgar's House, now incorporated into several of the shops on Staithe Street. Perched on the brow of the hill, it has a lookout facing the sea. When built, in 1740, its west front would not have faced a shopping street but rather the equally grand, but older, Newgates House.

In 1878, it was acquired by the Smith family of maltsters. They blocked up some of the west facing windows spending over £1000 on alterations. It is believed they named it after a shooting lodge in Scotland they knew. The huge garden was flanked to the west by a high wall behind which was a line of ilex trees. They opened it to the public for fêtes and tennis matches. In 1929, the death of its owner, Edgar Ladas Smith saw an end to such pursuits. Developed in the 1970s, the ground floor is now occupied by a pet store and a number of coffee shops, with apartments above.

South facing to catch the sun, the Normans is an example of late Georgian building (Shackle).

Normans' stables long disused in 1970 (Shackle).

Entrance 1970 (Shackle).

The Normans was built on the site of several cottages, in 1793, by John Bloom. He came from a family of seafarers, and later, ship owners and merchants of the town, going back to the early 17th century.

Bloom fell on hard times, and in 1833, the house was sold to one of a family of doctors, all confusingly named Hugh Rump. Used as a surgery, it was passed on to a succession of doctors and medical officers of health, ending with the retirement of Dr. 'Willie' Hicks in 1969. The loss of the surgery was one of the reasons that the Health Centre was built, a couple of hundred yards away.

Its garden was then made into a close of houses called Invaders Court. Each house is named after an invader, some of whom, like 'Scots', were unsuccessful.

The Normans, now part of a close of houses 2020 (Gower).

Bishop Ingle House in 1970 when it was still a clergy holiday home (Shackle).

Marsh House on Marsh Lane (Tipler).

74

The Lawn, now Bishop Ingle House, on Clubbs Lane was for a long time the house of a member of one of the two solicitors' families—E.B. Loynes and Sons. For a short while it was known as Bank House as it was the location of the earliest banking facilities in the town.

Before that, the Gales family ran an adjoining plant nursery. The house dates back to the 18th century and was for a long time owned by the absent Girdlestone family.

Its present name refers to its time as a clergy holiday home. It is now in private hands again.

Marsh House, built in 1742, lies on the north side of Church marsh. It was occupied by Hugh Rump, the first of a family of surgeons in the town and, much later, by another surgeon, Alfred Whitlock who was also registrar of births, marriage and deaths. It was bought by George Smith, the maltster, and later still, by George Turner Cain, a significant town councillor and garage owner. It is now, in the process of substantial renovation to restore it to its former glory.

Blenheim House, at the western end of the town overlooking the west marsh, is of the same period. Rump moved there in 1811. It was briefly a boarding school in the 1860s, and was later the residence of one of the Loynes family.

Some buildings defy attempts to identify their origins. One such is on Star Yard behind Staithe Street, a huge house probably dating back to the 17th century, but without any clues as to its origin or significance. Others like Elgar's House are not easily recognisable; part of it is a shop on Staithe Street. A row of outbuildings now forms Elgars Row which backs onto Shop Lane.

Among the many concealed buildings stands Westward House, probably originally Westward Ho! and set back from Mill Road just beyond the Buttlands. Among its many owners was Peter Hudson, a prominent miller in the town. He owned several of the windmills which stood along the ridge which runs to the west.

above: Blenheim House on Theatre Road.

below: Westward Ho! may date back to the 16th century when it would have been a farmhouse (Tipler).

left: The 'Manor House' on Star Yard 2020 (Arguile).

75

The Buttlands name might suggest the location of former archery butts. However, its more likely to be a piece of land 'abutting' the town. It became a fashionable place for the gentry to reside here. Its west side being developed towards the end of the Georgian period.

The Square House built in 1825 (Shackle).

The Buttlands' ownership was the cause of a long dispute between Wells Urban District Council and the Holkham Estate. The deeds were handed over to the Council in 1937. The building of fashionable town houses began around 1820. The Square House was built in 1825. Bought by the first of a line of surgeons in the town they moved from Blenheim House (above). By the 1860s it had become the favoured address of solicitors, doctors, merchants, maltsters, shopkeepers, shipowners and of two hotels, the *Crown* and the *Globe* (see p. 79). In 1897 a bandstand was built, frequently used, in early days, by the town's brass band, it survived until 1943. Monteagle, now flats, was, along with Clarence House, among the favoured shooting hotels advertising itself as the Buttlands Hotel.

The look of the Buttlands has not changed much over the years, but it is no longer the preferred place of residence for the business people of the town.

left: Buttlands from the north showing the bandstand pre-World War I (Tuck).

below: Monteagle east side of Buttlands 1970 (Shackle).

Public Houses

The Fleece with a model T Ford in the early part of the 20th century (McCallum).

The Bowling Green at the turn of the 20th century.

The Bowling Green in 1970 (Shackle).

Wells has had over fifty licensed premises over the years, though the highest number at any one time was 32. The tightening of regulations around the turn of the 20th century saw the number of outlets reduced to 16. Today there are but five. Many of the former public house buildings still remain.

Among the oldest still still serving is the *Bowling Green* opposite the church. It dates back at least to 1673. It has been almost continuously in business only closing briefly in the 1990s. The *Golden Fleece* is certainly ancient. Parts of the building date from Tudor times The plaster reliefs of St. Blaise and of the Viking invasions have been dated to 1710. It was, at one time, the centre of the town's civic activities: the magistrates' court and the harbour authorities both met there, until, the *Crown* opened in 1830. Stage coaches left from there until about the same time.

The two establishments on the Buttlands, the *Crown*, built in 1830 and the *Globe*, about the same period, remain in business.

The *Crown's* first landlord, Samuel Ellis, had transferred from the *Ostrich* (on Burnt Street) to take advantage of the growing importance of the Buttlands. He had previously owned the *Royal Standard* on the Quay. It became the venue for town meetings, the magistrates' court and the departure point for stage coaches. It was the preferred place for the gentry to stay. It encouraged cyclists.

The *Globe's* Assembly Rooms provided theatrical entertainment for the town in the late 19th century, after which, it fell on hard times, and was bought by Herbert Cawdron whose family ran it for many years. For a short time it was owned by Holkham Estate and, is now an independent operation. Its former Assembly Rooms have been converted into bed and breakfast accommodation.

The Cyclists Touring Club emblem can be seen above the main doorway of the Crown.

The Globe was run for many years by the Cawdron family.

The Crown in the 1920s.

79

The *Edinburgh*, at the top of High Street, was previously the *Leicester Arms* and, before that, the *Fighting Cocks*. It was renamed when rebuilt in 1897 by James Alexander Davidson, who also owned the *Fleece* and the *Crown*. He was also a coal merchant, a wine and spirit merchant and a cartridge manufacturer. As the *Fighting Cocks* it dates back to the 18th century and may be even older.

The Edinburgh in the 1970s (Shackle).

The Edinburgh 2012 (Hissey).

At the east end of Station Street is the variously named *Railway* and *Tinkers Hotel*, latterly the Lifeboat. It was built in 1845 to catch the anticipated railway traffic.

By the time it was taken over by Watneys in 1967, the railway had closed and was renamed the *Tinkers Hotel*. Becoming the *Lifeboat* in 1994 it closed in 2020.

The Railway Hotel at the turn of the century (Warren) Now the Lifeboat Inn with its sun room bricked in and a sloping roof 1990.

Of the many waterside pubs of yesteryear, the *Shipwrights* at the East End, was the last. It was a fisherman's pub, standing opposite the fishermen's cooperative. The ground outside, the so called

drying grounds, were widely used by families wishing to take advantage of its hospitality and the view. The upstairs room was, at one time, used by the Hydroplane Club for their meetings.

The *Ship*, at the opposite end of the Quay on Freeman Street (see p. 50), was also a local haunt. It closed in 1967 when the licence was transferred to the newly built *Ark Royal*. A popular pub for discos in this period, it struggled in the 21st century despite attempts to rebrand it, first as the *Captain's Table* and then as *Harleys*. In this incarnation it never actually opened and was demolished in 2020.

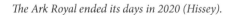

The Ark Royal ended its days in 2020 (Hissey).

above: The Shipwrights was a fishermen's pub (Warren).

left: The Shipwrights bar in the 1970s.

The Royal Standard, one of the oldest pubs in the town.

The number of buildings which were once licensed as public houses, inns or taverns are too numerous to record. Some of them though need a mention. The *Royal Standard*, now Standard House Chandlery, closed in 1905 as the authorities sought to reduce the number of licensed premises in the town. Dating back at least until the 18th century, Parson Woodforde stayed there in 1779. It was the place for public meetings, auctions of ships and the cargoes of wrecks, and an early departure point for stage coaches circa 1780.

The *Prince of Wales*, previously the *Tewkesbury Arms*, can be dated to 1868. It took the later name from a pub of that name in High Street which had closed. Closed in 1966, it is now a café.

The variously named *Six Ringers* and *Eight Ringers*, on Church Plain, like so many public houses in Wells was a Bullard's premises. The Norwich brewer was sold to Watneys in the 1960s and they closed it in 1971.

Standard House chandlery in 1970 when it was an antique shop (Shackle).

The Prince of Wales in the 1960s (Warren).

The Eight Ringers in the 1950s (Tuck).

The Vine ceased trading in 1965 and is now Angus House, a private residence.

Along the Quay there were at least eight public houses many of which there is no trace. Of the *Brewers Arms*, there is scarcely a photograph. Of the *Lord Nelson*, there are pictures: it lay approximately where Grays amusements were until the fire of 2005.

The *Sun Inn*, whose licence was not renewed in 1925, is now a restaurant and fish and chip shop, having been tea rooms for a while.

The *Vine* was one of five public houses on High Street, none of which remain, though the buildings are still extant. The *Duke's Head*, on the other side of the road, was a new building around 1870, replacing the *Green Dragon*, which went back at least to 1789. It closed in 1865.

The Lord Nelson (centre) was replaced by amusements.

The former Sun Inn, now a fish and chip and was a coffee shop in the 1970s.

Angus House

Churches

St Nicholas' Church

The Church before the fire of 1879.

There has probably been a church on this site since the conquest. Our first photograph shows the original medieval church, built about 1460. This building was destroyed, apart from the tower, in 1879, by fire. Rebuilt in 1883, it had to be substantially repaired in 1967.

Interior of rebuilt church

St Nicholas' Church choir 1929 (Tuck).

After the fire 1879.

Methodism

Methodists have been strong in Norfolk since their foundation in the 18th century. The Wesleyan Methodist chapel on Station Road opened in 1808 and the Primitive Methodist chapel on Theatre Road opened in 1891.

Reunification of the two branches in 1932 led to the closure of the Station Street Wesleyan chapel. It was bought by the Urban District Council in 1936 for use as the town's library. It opened in 1949.

The Theatre Road chapel became the Methodist chapel of the town.

The Primitive Methodist chapel on Theatre Road.

The Wesleyan chapel was converted into the town library (Shackle).

left: The Methodist chapel on Theatre Road (Shackle).

right: The Wesleyan Methodist chapel—1920.

85

The Friends' Meeting House on Church Street dates back to 1680, making it the oldest dissenting body in the town. It was enlarged in the early 19th century and later, taking part of the Wells workhouse site for its burial ground. After a period of decline, it revived in the 20th century due to the efforts of local councillor, Sam Peel.

The Congregational church on Clubbs Lane was built in 1817 and enlarged in 1826.

In 1928, The Roman Catholic Church was built on the Buttlands. Opened with great ceremony it was initially the subject of vandalism and graffiti.

Relations between churches now result in joint effort and occasional joint services.

The Quaker Meeting house in 1970 (Shackle).

Catholic consecration service 1928.

Wells Congregational Church (Shackle).

86

The consecration of the Roman Catholic Church in 1928.

Floods

1953

Over the centuries, high tides have led to flooding in Wells. In 1897 a vessel was left on the roadway at the east end.

The most devastating were the 1953 floods. The beach bank was breached in three places; houses on Freeman Street were awash, some having lost their outside walls; the Heacham railway line was washed away; the *Terra Nova* air sea rescue boat ended up on the Quay, together with other vessels. Over 300 people died along the coast, though none in Wells. A great number of domestic animals, sheep and cattle were drowned, their bodies lying bloated on the marshes for days. It was nine months before the breaches were finally filled and some kind of normality was restored to the town.

Over £16,000 was raised for the town to relieve the losses sustained by householders and shopkeepers.

After the 1897 flood.

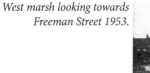

West marsh looking towards Freeman Street 1953.

top: *The backs of houses on Freeman Street 1953.*

bottom: *The remains of Pinewoods campsite 1953.*

Devastation on the Quay, on the beach and on the railway.

1978

Leisure cruisers lifted up on the Quay.

The northern breach in the beach bank.

The five hundred ton coaster Function on the Quay.

The 1978 flood was just as severe, though it produced much less damage. The beach bank was again breached, the houses were less severely damaged and the repairs were executed much more quickly. Leisure boats were lifted up and dumped on the Quay together with a coaster, the *Function*, whose removal presented a much bigger problem. A fishing boat, the *Strandline*, was carried through a breach. It came to rest on the fields beyond as the tide receded.

Helicopters were used to transport material from the Lime works to fill the breaches in the bank with little success; each tide was liable to wash away the work. It was the arrival of Dutch engineers, with pumping equipment, that enabled the breach to be filled. The caravan site was able to open by Whitsun (Spring) bank holiday, though it had looked pretty bleak.

It was obvious that the beach bank had to be raised and the harbour be improved. A moveable barrier across the west end of the Quay was constructed. This saved the houses on Freeman Street when another tidal surge took place in 2013.

Helicopter delivering lime from local works.

Heavy machinery working on the beach bank.

Piles to strengthen harbour wall 'in the 1980s.

Moveable barrier in place which saved the west end from inundation in 2013.

91

Index

THIS WAS FORMERLY A PORT CALLED BLAKENEY AND CLEY

Important Dates in the Maritime History of the Glaven Ports

Jonathan Hooton

A history of Blakeney and Cley by Jonathan Hooton.

David Stannard's facinating exploration of the lesser known history of Norfolk.

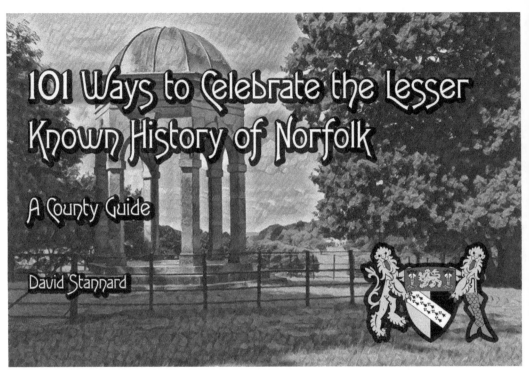

101 Ways to Celebrate the Lesser Known History of Norfolk

A County Guide

David Stannard

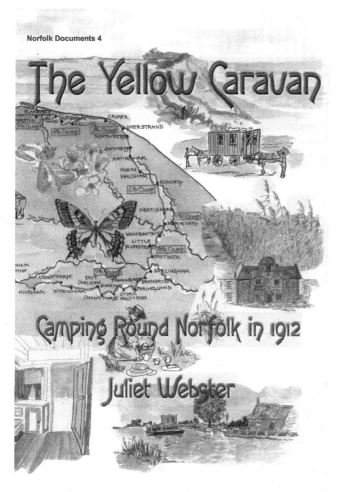

The Yellow Caravan

Camping Round Norfolk in 1912

Juliet Webster

Three Edwardian ladies take a caravanning trip around Norfolk in 1912.

Andy Reid looks at the grittier
side of Victorian Norfolk.

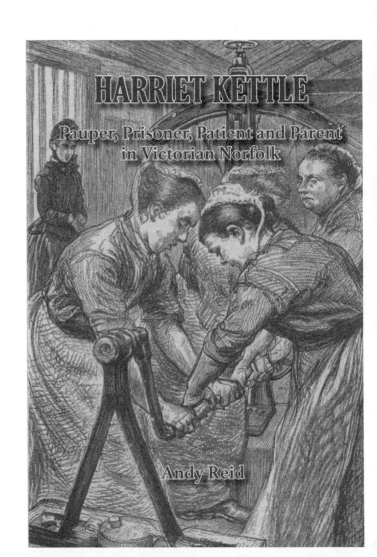

HARRIET KETTLE

Pauper, Prisoner, Patient and Parent
in Victorian Norfolk

Andy Reid

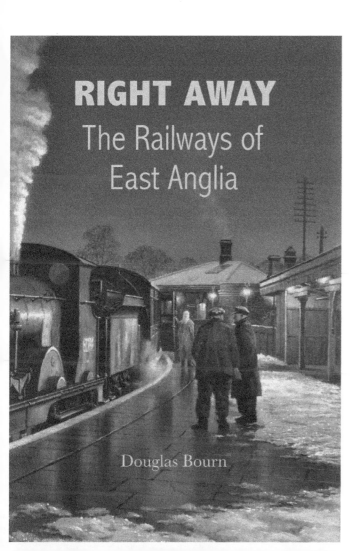

The history of East Anglia's railways.

The history of fruit growing in the
region with traditional recipes.

*Orchard Recipes from
Eastern England*

landscape, fruit and heritage

Monica Askay and Tom Williamson

EDWIN GOOCH

Champion of the Farmworkers

Simon Gooch

The biography of Norfolk Norfolk's MP and Chairman of the Labour Party.